SELECTED POEMS

POETRY

**The Collected Poems of
John Masefield**
In one volume

**The Collected Poems of
Maurice Baring**

Satirical Poems

Selected Poems

A Heart's Journey

Siegfried Sassoon

HEINEMANN

SELECTED POEMS

BY

SIEGFRIED SASSOON 1886-

WILLIAM HEINEMANN LTD
LONDON :: **TORONTO**

First published April 1925
Reprinted October 1927
September 1929, *September* 1930
November 1931, *November* 1933
January 1935, *February* 1936
May 1937

PRINTED IN GREAT BRITAIN AT THE WINDMILL PRESS
KINGSWOOD, SURREY

CONTENTS

CONTENTS

CONTENTS

COME in this hour to set my spirit free
When earth is no more mine though night goes out,
And stretching forth these arms I cannot be
Lord of winged sunrise and dim Arcady:
When fieldward boys far off with clack and shout
From orchards scare the birds in sudden rout,
Come, ere my heart grows cold and full of doubt
In the still summer dawns that waken me.

When the first lark goes up to look for day
And morning glimmers out of dreams, come then
Out of the songless valleys, over gray
Wide misty lands to bring me on my way:
For I am lone, a dweller among men
Hungered for what my heart shall never say.

1909

WHERE have you been, South Wind, this May-day morning?
With larks aloft, or skimming with the swallow,
Or with blackbirds in a green, sun-glinted thicket?

O, I heard you like a tyrant in the valley;
Your ruffian haste shook the young blossoming orchards;
You clapped rude hands, hallooing round the chimney,
And white your pennons streamed along the river.

You have robbed the bee, South Wind, in your adventure,
Blustering with gentle flowers; but I forgave you
When you stole to me shyly with scent of hawthorn.

1914

OLD English songs, you bring to me
A simple sweetness somewhat kin
To birds that through the mystery
Of earliest morn make tuneful din,
While hamlet steeples sleepily
At cock-crow chime out three and four,
Till maids get up betime and go,
With faces like the red sun low,
Clattering about the dairy floor.

1908

For Morn, my dome of blue,
For Meadows, green and gay,
And Birds who love the twilight of the leaves,
Let Jesus keep me joyful when I pray.

For the big Bees that hum
And hide in bells of flowers;
For the winding roads that come
To Evening's holy door,
May Jesus bring me grateful to his arms,
And guard my innocence for evermore.

1914

WHEN meadows are grey with the morn
In the dusk of the woods it is night;
The oak and the beech and the pine
War with the glimmer of light.

Dryads brown as the leaf
Move in the gloom of the glade;
When meadows are grey with the morn
Dim night in the wood has delayed.

The cocks that crow to the land
Are faint and hollow and shrill:
Dryads brown as the leaf
Whisper, and hide, and are still.

1910

WHEN old Noah stared across the floods
Sky and water melted into one
Looking-glass of shifting tides and sun.

Mountain-tops were few: the ship was foul:
All the morn old Noah marvelled greatly
At this weltering world that shone so stately,
Drowning deep the rivers and the plains.
Through the stillness came a rippling breeze;
Noah sighed, remembering the green trees.

Clear along the morning stooped a bird,—
Lit beside him with a blossomed sprig.
Earth was saved; and Noah danced a jig.

1915

I HEARD the farm cocks crowing, loud, and faint, and thin,
When hooded night was going and one clear planet winked:
I heard shrill notes begin down the spired wood distinct,
When cloudy shoals were chinked and gilt with fires of day.
White-misted was the weald; the lawns were silver-grey;
The lark his lonely field for heaven had forsaken;
And the wind upon its way whispered the boughs of may,
And touched the nodding peony-flowers to bid them waken.

1915

YE hooded witches, baleful shapes that moan,
Quench your fantastic lanterns and be still;
For now the moon through heaven sails alone,
Shedding her peaceful rays from hill to hill.
The faun from out his dim and secret place
Draws nigh the darkling pool and from his dream
Half-wakens, seeing there his sylvan face
Reflected, and the wistful eyes that gleam.

To his cold lips he sets the pipe to blow
Some drowsy note that charms the listening air:
The dryads from their trees come down and creep
Near to his side; monotonous and low,
He plays and plays till all the woodside there
Stirs to the voice of everlasting sleep.

1911

WHEN in your sober mood my body ye have laid
In sight and sound of things beloved, woodland and stream,
And the green turf has hidden the poor bones ye deem
No more a close companion with those rhymes we made;

Then, if some bird should pipe, or breezes stir the glade,
Thinking them for the while my voice, so let them seem
A fading message from the misty shores of dream,
Or wheresoever, following Death, my feet have strayed.

1908

In this meadow starred with spring
Shepherds kneel before their king.
Mary throned, with dreaming eyes,
Gowned in blue like rain-washed skies,
Lifts her tiny son that he
May behold their courtesy.
And green-smocked children, awed and good,
Bring him blossoms from the wood.

Clear the sunlit steeples chime
Mary's coronation-time.
Loud the happy children quire
To the golden-windowed morn;
While the lord of their desire
Sleeps below the crimson thorn.

1915

THERE stood a Poplar, tall and straight;
The fair, round Moon, uprisen late,
Made the long shadow on the grass
A ghostly bridge 'twixt heaven and me.
    But May, with slumbrous nights, must pass;
    And blustering winds will strip the tree.
And I've no magic to express
The moment of that loveliness;
So from these words you'll never guess
The stars and lilies I could see.

1916

THE glorying forest shakes and swings with glancing
Of boughs that dip and strain; young, slanting sprays
Beckon and shift like lissom creatures dancing,
While the blown beechwood streams with drifting rays.

Rooted in steadfast calm, grey stems are seen
Like weather-beaten masts; the wood, unfurled,
Seems as a ship with crowding sails of green
That sweeps across the lonely billowing world.

O luminous and lovely! Let your flowers,
Your ageless-squadroned wings, your surge and gleam,
Drown me in quivering brightness: let me fade
In the warm, rustling music of the hours
That guard your ancient wisdom: till my dream
Moves with the chant and whisper of the glade.

1916

WHEN half the drowsy world's a-bed
And misty morning rises red,
With jollity of horn and lusty cheer
Young Nimrod urges on his dwindling rout;
Along the yellowing coverts we can hear
His horse's hoofs thud hither and about:
In mulberry coat he rides and makes
Huge clamour in the sultry brakes.

1913

WHEN Wisdom tells me that the world's a speck
Lost on the shoreless blue of God's To-Day. . . .
I smile and think, "For every man his way:
The world's my ship, and I'm alone on deck!"

And when he tells me that the world's a spark
Lit in the whistling gloom of God's To-Night. . . .
I look within me to the edge of dark,
And dream, "The world's my field, and I'm the lark,
Alone with upward song, alone with light!"

1915

I'VE listened: and all the sounds I heard
Were music,—wind, and stream, and bird.
With youth who sang from hill to hill
I've listened: my heart is hungry still.

I've looked: the morning world was green;
Bright roofs and towers of town I've seen,
And stars, wheeling through wingless night.
I've looked: and my soul yet longs for light.

I've thought: but in my sense survives
Only the impulse of those lives
That were my making. Hear me say
"I've thought!"—and darkness hides my day.

I LIVED my days apart,
Dreaming fair songs for God,
By the glory in my heart
Covered and crowned and shod.

Now God is in the strife,
And I must seek Him there
Where death outnumbers life
And fury smites the air.

I walk the secret way
With anger in my brain.
O music through my clay,
When will you sound again?

1916

Give me your hand, my brother; search my face;
Look in these eyes lest I should think of shame.
For we have made an end of all things base;
We are returning by the road we came.

Your lot is with the ghosts of soldiers dead,
And I am in the field where men must fight.
But in the gloom I see your laurell'd head,
And through your victory I shall win the light.

1915

Music of whispering trees
Hushed by a broad-winged breeze
Where shaken water gleams;
And evening radiance falling
With reedy bird-notes calling.
O bear me safe through dark, you low-voiced streams.

I have no need to pray
That fear may pass away;
I scorn the growl and rumble of the fight
That summons me from cool
Silence of marsh and pool
And yellow lilies islanded in light.
O river of stars and shadows, lead me through the night.

1916

WHEN I'm among a blaze of lights,
With tawdry music and cigars
And women dawdling through delights,
And officers at cocktail bars,—
Sometimes I think of garden nights
And elm trees nodding at the stars.

I dream of a small firelit room
With yellow candles burning straight,
And glowing pictures in the gloom,
And kindly books that hold me late.
Of things like these I love to think
When I can never be alone:
Then someone says, "Another drink?"—
And turns my living heart to stone.

1916

SOLDIERS are citizens of death's gray land,
  Drawing no dividend from time's to-morrows.
In the great hour of destiny they stand,
  Each with his feuds and jealousies and sorrows.
Soldiers are sworn to action; they must win
  Some flaming fatal climax with their lives.
Soldiers are dreamers; when the guns begin
  They think of firelit homes, clean beds, and wives.

I see them in foul dug-outs, gnawed by rats,
  And in the ruined trenches, lashed with rain,
Dreaming of things they did with balls and bats,
  And mocked by hopeless longing to regain
Bank-holidays, and picture shows, and spats,
  And going to the office in the train.

1917

So Davies wrote: "This leaves me in the pink."
Then scrawled his name: "Your loving sweetheart, Willie."
With crosses for a hug. He'd had a drink
Of rum and tea; and, though the barn was chilly,
For once his blood ran warm; he had pay to spend.
Winter was passing; soon the year would mend.

He couldn't sleep that night. Stiff in the dark
He groaned and thought of Sundays at the farm,
When he'd go out as cheerful as a lark
In his best suit to wander arm-in-arm
With brown-eyed Gwen, and whisper in her ear
The simple, silly things she liked to hear.

And then he thought: to-morrow night we trudge
Up to the trenches, and my boots are rotten.
Five miles of stodgy clay and freezing sludge,
And everything but wretchedness forgotten.
To-night he's in the pink; but soon he'll die.
And still the war goes on; *he* don't know why.

1916

DARKNESS: the rain sluiced down; the mire was deep;
It was past twelve on a mid-winter night,
When peaceful folk in beds lay snug asleep:
There, with much work to do before the light,
We lugged our clay-sucked boots as best we might
Along the trench; sometimes a bullet sang,
And droning shells burst with a hollow bang;
We were soaked, chilled and wretched, every one.
Darkness: the distant wink of a huge gun.

I turned in the black ditch, loathing the storm;
A rocket fizzed and burned with blanching flare,
And lit the face of what had been a form
Floundering in mirk. He stood before me there;
I say that he was Christ; stiff in the glare,
And leaning forward from his burdening task,
Both arms supporting it; his eyes on mine
Stared from the woeful head that seemed a mask
Of mortal pain in Hell's unholy shine.

No thorny crown, only a woollen cap
He wore—an English soldier, white and strong,
Who loved his time like any simple chap,
Good days of work and sport and homely song;
Now he has learned that nights are very long,
And dawn a watching of the windowed sky.
But to the end, unjudging, he'll endure
Horror and pain, not uncontent to die
That Lancaster on Lune may stand secure.

He faced me, reeling in his weariness,
Shouldering his load of planks, so hard to bear.
I say that he was Christ, who wrought to bless
All groping things with freedom bright as air,
And with His mercy washed and made them fair
Then the flame sank, and all grew black as pitch,
While we began to struggle along the ditch;
And some one flung his burden in the muck,
Mumbling: "O Christ Almighty, now I'm stuck!"

1916

"Pass it along, the wiring party's going out"—
And yawning sentries mumble, "Wirers going out."
Unravelling; twisting; hammering stakes with muffled thud,
They toil with stealthy haste and anger in their blood.

The Boche sends up a flare. Black forms stand rigid there
Stock-still like posts; then darkness, and the clumsy ghosts
Stride thither and thither, whispering, tripped by clutching
  snare
Of snags and tangles.
     Ghastly dawn with vaporous coasts
Gleams desolate along the sky, night's misery ended.

Young Hughes was badly hit; I heard him carried away,
Moaning at every lurch; no doubt he'll die to-day.
But *we* can say the front-line wire's been safely mended.

1917

THREE hours ago he blundered up the trench,
Sliding and poising, groping with his boots;
Sometimes he tripped and lurched against the walls
With hands that pawed the sodden bags of chalk.
He couldn't see the man who walked in front;
Only he heard the drum and rattle of feet
Stepping along the trench-boards,—often splashing
Wretchedly where the sludge was ankle-deep.

Voices would grunt, "Keep to your right,—make way!"
When squeezing past the men from the front-line:
White faces peered, puffing a point of red;
Candles and braziers glinted through the chinks
And curtain-flaps of dug-outs; then the gloom
Swallowed his sense of sight; he stooped and swore
Because a sagging wire had caught his neck.
A flare went up; the shining whiteness spread
And flickered upward, showing nimble rats,
And mounds of glimmering sand-bags, bleached with rain
Then the slow, silver moment died in dark.

The wind came posting by with chilly gusts
And buffeting at corners, piping thin
And dreary through the crannies; rifle-shots
Would split and crack and sing along the night,
And shells came calmly through the drizzling air
To burst with hollow bang below the hill.

Three hours ago he stumbled up the trench;
Now he will never walk that road again:
He must be carried back, a jolting lump
Beyond all need of tenderness and care;
A nine-stone corpse with nothing more to do.

He was a young man with a meagre wife
And two pale children in a Midland town;
He showed the photograph to all his mates;
And they considered him a decent chap
Who did his work and hadn't much to say,
And always laughed at other people's jokes
Because he hadn't any of his own.
That night, when he was busy at his job
Of piling bags along the parapet,
He thought how slow time went, stamping his feet,
And blowing on his fingers, pinched with cold.

He thought of getting back by half-past twelve,
And tot of rum to send him warm to sleep
In draughty dug-out frowsty with the fumes
Of coke, and full of snoring, weary men.

He pushed another bag along the top,
Craning his body outward; then a flare
Gave one white glimpse of No Man's Land and wire;
And as he dropped his head the instant split
His startled life with lead, and all went out.

1916

I'D been on duty from two till four.
I went and stared at the dug-out door.
Down in the frowst I heard them snore.
"Stand-to!" Somebody grunted and swore.
     Dawn was misty; the skies were still;
     Larks were singing, discordant, shrill;
     They seemed happy; but *I* felt ill.
Deep in water I splashed my way
Up the trench to our bogged front line.
Rain had fallen the whole damned night.
O Jesus, send me a wound to-day,
And I'll believe in Your bread and wine,
And get my bloody old sins washed white!

1916

THE Bishop tells us: "When the boys come back
They will not be the same; for they'll have fought
In a just cause: they lead the last attack
On Anti-Christ; their comrade's blood has bought
New right to breed an honourable race.
They have challenged Death and dared him face to face."

"We're none of us the same!" the boys reply.
"For George lost both his legs; and Bill's stone blind;
Poor Jim's shot through the lungs and like to die;
And Bert's gone syphilitic: you'll not find
A chap who's served that hasn't found *some* change."
And the Bishop said: "The ways of God are strange!"

1916

IF I were fierce and bald and short of breath,
  I'd live with scarlet Majors at the Base,
And speed glum heroes up the line to death.
  You'd see me with my puffy petulant face,
Guzzling and gulping in the best hotel,
  Reading the Roll of Honour. "Poor young chap,"
I'd say—"I used to know his father well;
  Yes, we've lost heavily in this last scrap."
And when the war is done and youth stone dead
I'd toddle safely home and die—in bed.

1917

THE House is crammed: tier beyond tier they grin
And cackle at the Show, while prancing ranks
Of harlots shrill the chorus, drunk with din;
"We're sure the Kaiser loves the dear old Tanks!"

I'd like to see a Tank come down the stalls,
Lurching to rag-time tunes, or "Home, sweet Home,"—
And there'd be no more jokes in music-halls
To mock the riddled corpses round Bapaume.

1916

"Good-morning; good-morning!" the General said
When we met him last week on our way to the Line.
Now the soldiers he smiled at are most of 'em dead,
And we're cursing his staff for incompetent swine.
"He's a cheery old card," grunted Harry to Jack
As they slogged up to Arras with rifle and pack.

*   *   *

But he did for them both by his plan of attack.

1917

SHAKEN from sleep, and numbed and scarce awake,
Out in the trench with three hours' watch to take,
I blunder through the splashing mirk; and then
Hear the gruff muttering voices of the men
Crouching in cabins candle-chinked with light.
Hark! There's the big bombardment on our right
Rumbling and bumping; and the dark's a glare
Of flickering horror in the sectors where
We raid the Boche; men waiting, stiff and chilled,
Or crawling on their bellies through the wire.
"What? Stretcher-bearers wanted? Some one killed?"
Five minutes ago I heard a sniper fire:
Why did he do it? . . . Starlight overhead—
Blank stars. I'm wide-awake; and some chap's dead.

1917

THE DUG-OUT

Why do you lie with your legs ungainly huddled,
And one arm bent across your sullen cold
Exhausted face? It hurts my heart to watch you,
Deep-shadow'd from the candle's guttering gold:
And you wonder why I shake you by the shoulder;
Drowsy, you mumble and sigh and shift your head . . .
You are too young to fall asleep for ever;
And when you sleep you remind me of the dead.

1918

Down in the hollow there's the whole Brigade
Camped in four groups: through twilight falling slow
I hear a sound of mouth-organs, ill-played,
And murmur of voices, gruff, confused, and low.
Crouched among thistle-tufts I've watched the glow
Of a blurred orange sunset flare and fade;
And I'm content. To-morrow we must go
To take some cursed Wood. . . . O world God made!

1916

AT dawn the ridge emerges massed and dun
In the wild purple of the glowering sun
Smouldering through spouts of drifting smoke that shroud
The menacing scarred slope; and, one by one,
Tanks creep and topple forward to the wire.
The barrage roars and lifts. Then, clumsily bowed
With bombs and guns and shovels and battle-gear,
Men jostle and climb to meet the bristling fire.
Lines of grey, muttering faces, masked with fear,
They leave their trenches, going over the top,
While time ticks blank and busy on their wrists,
And hope, with furtive eyes and grappling fists,
Flounders in mud. O Jesu, make it stop!

1917

WE'D gained our first objective hours before
While dawn broke like a face with blinking eyes,
Pallid, unshaved and thirsty, blind with smoke.
Things seemed all right at first. We held their line,
With bombers posted, Lewis guns well placed,
And clink of shovels deepening the shallow trench.
The place was rotten with dead; green clumsy legs
High-booted, sprawled and grovelled along the saps;
And trunks, face downward in the sucking mud,
Wallowed like trodden sand-bags loosely filled;
And naked sodden buttocks, mats of hair,
Bulged, clotted heads, slept in the plastering slime.
And then the rain began,—the jolly old rain!

A yawning soldier knelt against the bank,
Staring across the morning blear with fog;
He wondered when the Allemands would get busy;
And then, of course, they started with five-nines
Traversing, sure as fate, and never a dud.
Mute in the clamour of shells he watched them burst
Spouting dark earth and wire with gusts from hell,
While posturing giants dissolved in drifts of smoke.
He crouched and flinched, dizzy with galloping fear
Sick for escape,—loathing the strangled horror
And butchered, frantic gestures of the dead.

An officer came blundering down the trench:
"Stand-to and man the fire-step!" On he went . . .
Gasping and bawling, "Fire-step . . . counter-attack!"
Then the haze lifted. Bombing on the right
Down the old sap: machine-guns on the left;
And stumbling figures looming out in front.
"O Christ, they're coming at us!" Bullets spat,
And he remembered his rifle . . . rapid fire . . .
And started blazing wildly . . . then a bang
Crumpled and spun him sideways, knocked him out
To grunt and wriggle: none heeded him; he choked
And fought the flapping veils of smothering gloom.
Lost in a blurred confusion of yells and groans . . .
Down, and down, and down, he sank and drowned,
Bleeding to death. The counter-attack had failed.

1917

(Hindenburg Line, April 1917.)

GROPING along the tunnel, step by step,
He winked his prying torch with patching glare
From side to side, and sniffed the unwholesome air.

Tins, boxes, bottles, shapes too vague to know,
A mirror smashed, the mattress from a bed;
And he, exploring fifty feet below
The rosy gloom of battle overhead.

Tripping, he grabbed the wall; saw some one lie
Humped at his feet, half-hidden by a rug,
And stooped to give the sleeper's arm a tug.
"I'm looking for headquarters." No reply.
"God blast your neck!" (For days he'd had no sleep,)
"Get up and guide me through this stinking place."
Savage, he kicked a soft, unanswering heap,
And flashed his beam across the livid face
Terribly glaring up, whose eyes yet wore
Agony dying hard ten days before;
And fists of fingers clutched a blackening wound.

Alone he staggered on until he found
Dawn's ghost that filtered down a shafted stair
To the dazed, muttering creatures underground
Who hear the boom of shells in muffled sound.
At last, with sweat of horror in his hair,
He climbed through darkness to the twilight air,
Unloading hell behind him step by step.

1917   38

I KNEW a simple soldier boy
Who grinned at life in empty joy,
Slept soundly through the lonesome dark,
And whistled early with the lark.

In winter trenches, cowed and glum
With crumps and lice and lack of rum,
He put a bullet through his brain.
No one spoke of him again.

*   *   *

You smug-faced crowds with kindling eye
Who cheer when soldier lads march by,
Sneak home and pray you'll never know
The hell where youth and laughter go.

1917

REMORSE

Lost in the swamp and welter of the pit,
He flounders off the duck-boards; only he knows
Each flash and spouting crash,—each instant lit
When gloom reveals the streaming rain. He goes
Heavily, blindly on. And, while he blunders,
"Could anything be worse than this?"—he wonders,
Remembering how he saw those Germans run,
Screaming for mercy among the stumps of trees:
Green-faced, they dodged and darted: there was one
Livid with terror, clutching at his knees. . . .
Our chaps were sticking 'em like pigs. . . . "O hell!"
He thought—"there's things in war one dare not tell
Poor father sitting safe at home, who reads
Of dying heroes and their deathless deeds."

1917

Not much to me is yonder lane
    Where I go every day;
But when there's been a shower of rain
    And hedge-birds whistle gay,
I know my lad that's out in France
    With fearsome things to see
Would give his eyes for just one glance
    At our white hawthorn tree.

*   *   *

Not much to me is yonder lane
    Where *he* so longs to tread;
But when there's been a shower of rain
I think I'll never weep again
    Until I've heard he's dead.

1917

You love us when we're heroes, home on leave,
Or wounded in a mentionable place.
You worship decorations; you believe
That chivalry redeems the war's disgrace.
You make us shells. You listen with delight,
By tales of dirt and danger fondly thrilled.
You crown our distant ardours while we fight,
And mourn our laurelled memories when we're killed.

You can't believe that British troops 'retire'
When hell's last horror breaks them, and they run,
Trampling the terrible corpses—blind with blood.
O German mother dreaming by the fire,
While you are knitting socks to send your son
His face is trodden deeper in the mud.

1917

LAMENTATIONS

I FOUND him in a guard-room at the Base.
From the blind darkness I had heard his crying
And blundered in. With puzzled, patient face
A sergeant watched him; it was no good trying
To stop it; for he howled and beat his chest.
And, all because his brother had gone West,
Raved at the bleeding war; his rampant grief
Moaned, shouted, sobbed, and choked, while he was
    kneeling
Half-naked on the floor. In my belief
Such men have lost all patriotic feeling.

1917

"The effect of our bombardment was terrific. One man told
me he had never seen so many dead before."

War Correspondent.

"He'd never seen so many dead before."
They sprawled in yellow daylight while he swore
And gasped and lugged his everlasting load
Of bombs along what once had been a road.
"How peaceful are the dead."
Who put that silly gag in some one's head?

"He'd never seen so many dead before."
The lilting words danced up and down his brain,
While corpses jumped and capered in the rain.
No, no; he wouldn't count them any more . . .
The dead have done with pain:
They've choked; they can't come back to life again.

When Dick was killed last week he looked like that,
Flapping along the fire-step like a fish,
After the blazing crump had knocked him flat . . .
*"How many dead? As many as ever you wish,
Don't count 'em; they're too many.
Who'll buy my nice fresh corpses, two a penny?"*

1917

His wet white face and miserable eyes
Brought nurses to him more than groans and sighs:
But hoarse and low and rapid rose and fell
His troubled voice: he did the business well.

The ward grew dark; but he was still complaining,
And calling out for "Dickie." "Curse the Wood!
It's time to go; O Christ, and what's the good?—
We'll never take it; and it's always raining."

I wondered where he'd been; then heard him shout,
"They snipe like hell! O Dickie, don't go out" . . .
I fell asleep . . . next morning he was dead;
And some Slight Wound lay smiling on his bed.

1916

AUTUMN

OCTOBER's bellowing anger breaks and cleaves
The bronzed battalions of the stricken wood
In whose lament I hear a voice that grieves
For battle's fruitless harvest, and the feud
Of outraged men. Their lives are like the leaves
Scattered in flocks of ruin, tossed and blown
Along the westering furnace flaring red.
O martyred youth and manhood overthrown,
The burden of your wrongs is on my head.

1917

Hullo! here's my platoon, the lot I had last year.
"The War 'll be over soon."
                    "What 'opes?"
                              "No bloody fear!"
Then, "Number Seven, 'shun! All present and correct."
They're standing in the sun, impassive and erect.
Young Gibson with his grin; and Morgan, tired and white;
Jordan, who's out to win a D.C.M. some night:
And Hughes that's keen on wiring; and Davies ('79),
Who always must be firing at the Boche front line.

*   *   *

"Old soldiers never die; they simply fide a-why!"
That's what they used to sing along the roads last spring;
That's what they used to say before the push began;
That's where they are to-day, knocked over to a man.

1917

DOES it matter?—losing your legs? . . .
For people will always be kind,
And you need not show that you mind
When the others come in after football
To gobble their muffins and eggs.

Does it matter?—losing your sight? . . .
There's such splendid work for the blind;
And people will always be kind,
As you sit on the terrace remembering
And turning your face to the light.

Do they matter?—those dreams from the pit? . . .
You can drink and forget and be glad,
And people won't say that you're mad;
For they'll know that you've fought for your country,
And no one will worry a bit.

1917

WELL, how are things in Heaven? I wish you'd say,
 Because I'd like to know that you're all right.
Tell me, have you found everlasting day,
 Or been sucked in by everlasting night?
For when I shut my eyes your face shows plain;
 I hear you make some cheery old remark;
I can rebuild you in my brain,
 Though you've gone out patrolling in the dark.

You hated tours of trenches; you were proud
 Of nothing more than having good years to spend;
Longed to get home and join the careless crowd
 Of chaps who work in peace with Time for friend.
That's all washed out now. You're beyond the wire:
 No earthly chance can send you crawling back:
You've finished with machine-gun fire,
 Knocked over in a hopeless dud-attack.

Somehow I always thought you'd get done in,
 Because you were so desperate keen to live:
You were all out to try and save your skin,
 Well knowing how much the world had got to give.
You joked at shells and talked the usual "shop,"
 Stuck to your dirty job and did it fine:
With "Jesus Christ! when *will* it stop?
 Three years. . . . It's hell unless we break their line."

So when they told me you'd been left for dead
    I wouldn't believe them, feeling it *must* be true.
Next week the bloody Roll of Honour said
    "Wounded and missing"—(That's the thing to do
When lads are left in shell-holes dying slow,
    With nothing but blank sky and wounds that ache,
Moaning for water till they know
    It's night, and then it's not worth while to wake.)

*   *   *

Good-bye, old lad! Remember me to God,
    And tell Him that our Politicians swear
They won't give in till Prussian Rule's been trod
    Under the Heel of England. . . . Are you there? . . .
Yes . . . and the War won't end for at least two years;
But we've got stacks of men. . . . I'm blind with tears,
    Staring into the dark. Cheero!
I wish they'd killed you in a decent show.

1917

WHEN I'm asleep, dreaming and lulled and warm,—
They come, the homeless ones, the noiseless dead.
While the dim charging breakers of the storm
Bellow and drone and rumble overhead,
Out of the gloom they gather about my bed.
They whisper to my heart; their thoughts are mine.
"Why are you here with all your watches ended?
From Ypres to Frise we sought you in the Line."
In bitter safety I awake, unfriended;
And while the dawn begins with slashing rain
I think of the Battalion in the mud.
"When are you going out to them again?
Are they not still your brothers through our blood?"

1917

I AM banished from the patient men who fight.
They smote my heart to pity, built my pride.
Shoulder to aching shoulder, side by side,
They trudged away from life's broad wealds of light.
Their wrongs were mine; and ever in my sight
They went arrayed in honour. But they died,—
Not one by one: and mutinous I cried
To those who sent them out into the night.

The darkness tells how vainly I have striven
To free them from the pit where they must dwell
In outcast gloom convulsed and jagged and riven
By grappling guns. Love drove me to rebel.
Love drives me back to grope with them through hell;
And in their tortured eyes I stand forgiven.

1917

FROM you, Beethoven, Bach, Mozart,
    The substance of my dreams took fire.
You built cathedrals in my heart,
    And lit my pinnacled desire.
You were the ardour and the bright
    Procession of my thoughts toward prayer.
You were the wrath of storm, the light
    On distant citadels aflare.

Great names, I cannot find you now
    In these loud years of youth that strives
Through doom towards peace: upon my brow
    I wear a wreath of banished lives.
You have no part with lads who fought
    And laughed and suffered at my side.
Your fugues and symphonies have brought
    No memory of my friends who died.

For when my brain is on their track,
In slangy speech I call them back.
With fox-trot tunes their ghosts I charm.
"Another little drink won't do us any harm."
      I think of rag-time; a bit of rag-time;
      And see their faces crowding round
      To the sound of the syncopated beat.

They've got such jolly things to tell,
Home from hell with a Blighty wound so neat. . . .

*   *   *

And so the song breaks off; and I'm alone.
They're dead. . . . For God's sake stop that gramophone.

1917

Now light the candles; one; two; there's a moth;
What silly beggars they are to blunder in
And scorch their wings with glory, liquid flame—
No, no, not that,—it's bad to think of war
When thoughts you've gagged all day come back to scare you;
And it's been proved that soldiers don't go mad
Unless they lose control of ugly thoughts
That drive them out to jabber among the trees.

Now light your pipe; look, what a steady hand.
Draw a deep breath; stop thinking; count fifteen,
And you're as right as rain. . . .
                                        Why won't it rain? . . .
I wish there'd be a thunder-storm to-night,
With bucketsful of water to sluice the dark
And make the roses hang their dripping heads.

Books; what a jolly company they are,
Standing so quiet and patient on their shelves,
Dressed in dim brown, and black, and white, and green;
And every kind of colour. Which will you read?
Come on; O *do* read something; they're so wise.
I tell you all the wisdom of the world
Is waiting for you on those shelves; and yet
You sit and gnaw your nails, and let your pipe out,
And listen to the silence: on the ceiling
There's one big, dizzy moth that bumps and flutters;

And in the breathless air outside the house
The garden waits for something that delays.
There must be crowds of ghosts among the trees,—
Not people killed in battle,—they're in France,—
But horrible shapes in shrouds—old men who died
Slow, natural deaths,—old men with ugly souls,
Who wore their bodies out with nasty sins.

*   *   *

You're quiet and peaceful, summering safe at home;
You'd never think there was a bloody war on! . . .
O yes, you would . . . why, you can hear the guns.
Hark! Thud, thud, thud,—quite soft . . . they never cease—
Those whispering guns—O Christ, I want to go out
And screech at them to stop—I'm going crazy;
I'm going stark, staring mad because of the guns.

1917

No doubt they'll soon get well; the shock and strain
Have caused their stammering, disconnected talk.
Of course they're "longing to go out again,"—
These boys with old scared faces, learning to walk.
They'll soon forget their haunted nights; their cowed
Subjection to the ghosts of friends who died,—
Their dreams that drip with murder; and they'll be proud
Of glorious war that shatter'd all their pride . . .
Men who went out to battle, grim and glad;
Children, with eyes that hate you, broken and mad.

1917

E

(Great War)

SQUIRE nagged and bullied till I went to fight
(Under Lord Derby's scheme). I died in hell—
(They called it Passchendaele); my wound was slight,
And I was hobbling back, and then a shell
Burst slick upon the duck-boards; so I fell
Into the bottomless mud, and lost the light.

In sermon-time, while Squire is in his pew,
He gives my gilded name a thoughtful stare;
For though low down upon the list, I'm there:
"In proud and glorious memory"—that's my due.
Two bleeding years I fought in France for Squire;
I suffered anguish that he's never guessed;
Once I came home on leave; and then went west.
What greater glory could a man desire?

1918

(Egyptian Base Camp)

THEY are gathering round . . .
Out of the twilight; over the grey-blue sand,
Shoals of low-jargoning men drift inward to the sound,—
The jangle and throb of a piano . . . tum-ti-tum. . . .
Drawn by a lamp, they come
Out of the glimmering lines of their tents, over the shuffling
    sand.

O sing us the songs, the songs of our own land,
You warbling ladies in white.
Dimness conceals the hunger in our faces,
This wall of faces risen out of the night,
These eyes that keep their memories of the places
So long beyond their sight.

Jaded and gay, the ladies sing; and the chap in brown
Tilts his grey hat; jaunty and lean and pale,
He rattles the keys . . . some actor-bloke from town . . .
"God send you home"; and then *"A long, long trail";*
"I hear you calling me"; and *"Dixieland"* . . .
Sing slowly . . . now the chorus . . . one by one.
We hear them, drink them; till the concert's done.
Silent, I watch the shadowy mass of soldiers stand.
Silent, they drift away, over the glimmering sand.

1918

I stood with the Dead, so forsaken and still:
  When dawn was grey I stood with the Dead.
And my slow heart said, "You must kill; you must kill:
  Soldier, soldier, morning is red."

On the shapes of the slain in their crumpled disgrace
  I stared for a while through the thin cold rain. . .
"O lad that I loved, there is rain on your face,
  And your eyes are blurred and sick like the plain."

I stood with the Dead . . . They were dead; they were dead;
  My heart and my head beat a march of dismay:
And gusts of the wind came dulled by the guns . . .
  "Fall in!" I shouted; "Fall in for your pay!"

1918

HE drowsed and was aware of silence heaped
Round him, unshaken as the steadfast walls;
Aqueous like floating rays of amber light,
Soaring and quivering in the wings of sleep,
Silence and safety; and his mortal shore
Lipped by the inward moonless waves of death.

Some one was holding water to his mouth.
He swallowed, unresisting; moaned and dropped
Through crimson gloom to darkness; and forgot
The opiate throb and ache that was his wound.
Water—calm, sliding green above the weir;
Water—a sky-lit alley for his boat,
Bird-voiced, and bordered with reflected flowers
And shaken hues of summer: drifting down,
He dipped contented oars, and sighed, and slept.

Night, with a gust of wind, was in the ward,
Blowing the curtain to a glimmering curve.
Night. He was blind; he could not see the stars
Glinting among the wraiths of wandering cloud;
Queer blots of colour, purple, scarlet, green,
Flickered and faded in his drowning eyes.

Rain; he could hear it rustling through the dark;
Fragrance and passionless music woven as one;
Warm rain on drooping roses; pattering showers
That soak the woods; not the harsh rain that sweeps

Behind the thunder, but a trickling peace
Gently and slowly washing life away.

*   *   *

He stirred, shifting his body; then the pain
Leaped like a prowling beast, and gripped and tore
His groping dreams with grinding claws and fangs.
But some one was beside him; soon he lay
Shuddering because that evil thing had passed.
And Death, who'd stepped toward him, paused and stared.

Light many lamps and gather round his bed.
Lend him your eyes, warm blood, and will to live.
Speak to him; rouse him; you may save him yet.
He's young; he hated war; how should he die
When cruel old campaigners win safe through?

But Death replied: "I choose him." So he went,
And there was silence in the summer night;
Silence and safety; and the veils of sleep.
Then, far away, the thudding of the guns.

1916

In fifty years, when peace outshines
Remembrance of the battle lines,
Adventurous lads will sigh and cast
Proud looks upon the plundered past.
On summer morn or winter's night,
Their hearts will kindle for the fight,
Reading a snatch of soldier-song,
Savage and jaunty, fierce and strong;
And through the angry marching rhymes
Of blind regret and haggard mirth,
They'll envy us the dazzling times
When sacrifice absolved our earth.

Some ancient man with silver locks
Will lift his weary face to say:
"War was a fiend who stopped our clocks
Although we met him grim and gay."
And then he'll speak of Haig's last drive,
Marvelling that any came alive
Out of the shambles that men built
And smashed, to cleanse the world of guilt.
But the boys, with grim and sidelong glance,
Will think, "Poor grandad's day is done."
And dream of lads who fought in France
And lived in time to share the fun.

1917

RECONCILIATION

When you are standing at your hero's grave,
Or near some homeless village where he died,
Remember, through your heart's rekindling pride,
The German soldiers who were loyal and brave.

Men fought like brutes; and hideous things were done:
And you have nourished hatred, harsh and blind.
But in that Golgotha perhaps you'll find
The mothers of the men who killed your son.

1918

AFTERMATH

Have you forgotten yet? . . .

For the world's events have rumbled on since those gagged
days,

Like traffic checked awhile at the crossing of city ways:

And the haunted gap in your mind has filled with thoughts
that flow

Like clouds in the lit heaven of life; and you're a man reprieved
to go,

Taking your peaceful share of Time, with joy to spare.

But the past is just the same,—and War's a bloody game. . . .

Have you forgotten yet? . . .

*Look down, and swear by the slain of the War that you'll never
forget.*

Do you remember the dark months you held the sector at
Mametz,—

The nights you watched and wired and dug and piled sandbags
on parapets?

Do you remember the rats; and the stench

Of corpses rotting in front of the front-line trench,—

And dawn coming, dirty-white, and chill with a hopeless
rain?

Do you ever stop and ask, "Is it all going to happen again?"

Do you remember that hour of din before the attack,—

And the anger, the blind compassion that seized and shook
you then

As you peered at the doomed and haggard faces of your men?
Do you remember the stretcher-cases lurching back
With dying eyes and lolling heads,—those ashen-grey
Masks of the lads who once were keen and kind and gay?

Have you forgotten yet? . . .
*Look up, and swear by the green of the Spring that you'll never
forget.*

1919

WHEN I was young my heart and head were light,
And I was gay and feckless as a colt
Out in the fields, with morning in the may,
Wind on the grass, wings in the orchard bloom.
    O thrilling sweet, my joy, when life was free,
    And all the paths led on from hawthorn-time
    Across the carolling meadows into June.

But now my heart is heavy-laden. I sit
Burning my dreams away beside the fire;
And I am rich in all that I have lost.
    O starshine on the fields of long-ago,
    Bring me the darkness and the nightingale;
    Dim wealds of vanished summer, peace of home,
    And silence: and the faces of my friends.

1919

Splashing along the boggy woods all day,
And over brambled hedge and holding clay,
I shall not think of him:
But when the watery fields grow brown and dim,
And hounds have lost their fox, and horses tire,
I know that he'll be with me on my way
Home through the darkness to the evening fire.

He's jumped each stile along the glistening lanes;
His hand will be upon the mud-soaked reins;
Hearing the saddle creak,
He'll wonder if the frost will come next week.
I shall forget him in the morning light;
And while we gallop on he will not speak:
But at the stable-door he'll say good-night.

1917

THEY know not the green leaves;
In whose earth-haunting dream
Dimly the forest heaves
And voiceless goes the stream.
Strangely they seek a place
In love's night-memoried hall;
Peering from face to face,
Until some heart shall call
And keep them, for a breath.
Half-mortal . . . (*Hark to the rain!*) . . .
They are dead . . . (*O hear how death
Gropes on the shutter'd pane!*)

1918

ADAM, a brown old vulture in the rain,
Shivered below his wind-whipped olive-trees;
Huddling sharp chin on scarred and scraggy knees,
He moaned and mumbled to his darkening brain;
"*He was the grandest of them all—was Cain!*
"A lion laired in the hills, that none could tire:
"Swift as a stag: a stallion of the plain,
"Hungry and fierce with deeds of huge desire."

Grimly he thought of Abel, soft and fair—
A lover with disaster in his face,
And scarlet blossom twisted in bright hair.
"Afraid to fight; was murder more disgrace? . . .
"*God always hated Cain*" . . . He bowed his head—
The gaunt wild man whose lovely sons were dead.

1918

COME down from heaven to meet me when my breath
Chokes, and through drumming shafts of stifling death
I stumble toward escape, to find the door
Opening on morn where I may breathe once more
Clear cock-crow airs across some valley dim
With whispering trees. While dawn along the rim
Of night's horizon flows in lakes of fire,
Come down from heaven's bright hill, my song's desire.

Belov'd and faithful, teach my soul to wake
In glades deep-ranked with flowers that gleam and shake
And flock your paths with wonder. In your gaze
Show me the vanquished vigil of my days.
Mute in that golden silence hung with green,
Come down from heaven and bring me in your eyes
Remembrance of all beauty that has been,
And stillness from the pools of Paradise.

1917

IDYLL

In the grey summer garden I shall find you
With day-break and the morning hills behind you.
There will be rain-wet roses; stir of wings;
And down the wood a thrush that wakes and sings.
Not from the past you'll come, but from that deep
Where beauty murmurs to the soul asleep:
And I shall know the sense of life re-born
From dreams into the mystery of morn
Where gloom and brightness meet. And standing there
Till that calm song is done, at last we'll share
The league-spread quiring symphonies that are
Joy in the world, and peace, and dawn's one star.

1918

SLEEP; and my song shall build about your bed
A Paradise of dimness. You shall feel
The folding of tired wings; and peace will dwell
Throned in your silence; and one hour shall hold
Summer, and midnight, and immensity
Lulled to forgetfulness. For where you dream
The stately gleam of foliage shall embower
Your slumbering thought with tapestries of blue.
And there shall be no memory of the sky,
Nor sunlight with its cruelty of swords.
But, to your soul that sinks from deep to deep
Through drowned and glimmering colour, time shall be
Only slow rhythmic swaying; and your breath;
And roses in the darkness: and my love.

1918

I love all things that pass: their briefness is
Music that fades on transient silences.
Winds, birds, and glittering leaves that flare and fall—
They fling delight across the world; they call
To rhythmic-flashing limbs that rove and race . . .

    A moment in the dawn for Youth's lit face;
    A moment's passion, closing on the cry—
    "O Beauty, born of lovely things that die!"

1918

EVERYONE suddenly burst out singing;
And I was filled with such delight
As prisoned birds must find in freedom
Winging wildly across the white
Orchards and dark green fields; on; on; and out of sight.

Everyone's voice was suddenly lifted,
And beauty came like the setting sun.
My heart was shaken with tears, and horror
Drifted away. . . . O but every one
Was a bird; and the song was wordless; the singing will never
be done.

1919